™

Whose Clues?

By
Nathan Levy

MIND
MOTION™

TREND enterprises, Inc.

Introduction

What better way to provide a fun, change of pace than with a Whose Clues?™ book! Not only do you have fun trying to guess the answer, but also you are developing creative, divergent thinking skills.

Each page gives five clues that describe a famous person or character. By listening to each of the clues, asking questions, and working together, players guess the person's or character's identity. Participants will have many chances to develop cooperative learning and deductive thinking skills—without even realizing it. Whose Clues?™ provides unlimited teaching and learning opportunities that kids from ages 8 to 88 love!

How to Use This Book

1. The object is to identify the person or character described by the clues.

2. Choose a reader to read the first clue. Always read only one clue at a time.

3. Remind the players to listen carefully to the clue. After hearing the clue they may ask "yes" or "no" questions and work together to figure out the answer. Answer their questions only with "yes" or "no" responses. Allow adequate time for the questions.

4. Read the next clue and repeat the process until all the clues have been read, or until someone correctly identifies the person or character.

5. If the players are clearly stuck and frustrated after several repetitions, feel free to give them hints.

Who am I?

- If my home were alive, it would be a ballerina.

- I proudly served the U.S.

- In one of my musical arrangements, a person was begged to be kind.

- A type of music became more popular because of the way my hips moved.

- I was the king of Rock and Roll.

1

Who am I?

- I started singing in my church choir.

- I sang for a deceased King.

- My voice was declared to be one of Michigan's natural resources..

- I was the first female voted into the Rock and Roll Hall of Fame.

- All I want is *RESPECT*.

Aretha Franklin

2

who am I?

- I was successful before Elvis Presley.

- I helped popularize the piano.

- "My" movie was very successful.

- Most people did not know my first name.

- I was one of the youngest classical composers ever.

3 Wolfgang Amadeus Mozart

Who am I?

- What a voice I had!
- *Strangers in the Night*
- *New York, New York*
- Chairman of the Board
- *My Way*

Frank Sinatra

4

Who am I?

- I would never try to run for President, because I couldn't win.

- I'd do *Anything for You.*

- People love to *Conga* to my music.

- My Latin Boys became a Sound Machine.

- I am the "Queen of Latin Pop."

5

Gloria Estefan

Who am I?

- I was one of three.

- Michigan was my home.

- Motown was my label.

- *Stop! In the Name of Love*

- My group reigned supreme.

Diana Ross,
of The Supremes

6

Who am I?

- I was born in Bonn in the 18th century.

- Snoopy and I have something in common.

- I was deaf.

- Dum dum da dum

- My *5th Symphony* is recognized worldwide.

7

Ludwig van Beethoven

Who am I?

- I attended the University of Michigan.

- I was in a *League of their Own.*

- I made *Vogue* popular.

- *You Must Love Me*

- My parents gave me the name Madonna Louise Veronica Ciccone.

Madonna

8

who am I?

- One of my songs talks about my birthplace.

- I was *Born to Run.*

- My band is found between D Street and F Street.

- I was *Born in the USA.*

- My fans call me the Boss.

Bruce Springsteen

Who am I?

- We have obvious similarities as performers.

- We have never performed a duet.

- Dark glasses characterize one of our similarities.

- Playing the piano is another thing we both do.

- *Hit the Road Jack* and *Isn't She Lovely* are two separate hits of ours.

Ray Charles and Stevie Wonder

10

Who am I?

- We crawled.

- We all lived underwater.

- We remembered the past.

- We invaded America in 1964.

- Best known as four misspelled bugs.

11

Who am I?

- I was born in Germany.

- A tree is featured in an Americanized version of my music.

- Adults hum my music.

- Babies relax to it.

- My lullaby is world famous.

Who am I?

- I was a great crooner.

- Swing, Thing, Ring,
  _____

- On the Road with Great Hope

- A snowy Christmas makes me dream.

- My real name was Harry Lillis Crosby.

Who am I?

- I'm famous for my continual motion.

- Counterpoint is my trademark.

- J.S.

- Black and white were keys to my fame.

- Step back (Bach). The train is coming.

Who am I?

- I won my first song and dance competition when I was five years old.

- I sang at Dallas Cowboys games.

- I'm not *Blue* about my future.

- I remind people of Patsy Cline.

- My name rhymes with times.

15

LeAnn Rimes

Who am I?

- Beethoven said I was the greatest composer who ever lived.

- The name of my music came from the Lord.

- Get a hold of it.

- It tips a teapot.

- My favorite work was *The Messiah*.

George Frederick Handel

16

Who am I?

- I've been imitated by many.

- I have performed with some of the greatest jazz musicians.

- My sound and my nickname are exclusive.

- *Hello Dolly!*

- I share my last name with the first man to walk on the moon.

17

Louis Armstrong

Who am I?

- People don't think of me as a composer.

- Old Blue Eyes has the same first name.

- The War of 1812

- Every professional baseball game

- Twilight's last gleaming

who am I?

- I live near the home of the football Vikings.

- I record in a park that has a pattern.

- *Batman* plays my music.

- I'm known for the color of my reign.

- I gave up my name for a sign you can't pronounce.

The Artist (formerly known as Prince)

Who am I?

- I was a soloist in the New Hope Baptist Junior Choir when I was eleven.

- My debut album was the biggest selling of all time.

- I was a top junior model and appeared on the covers of *Glamour* and *Seventeen*.

- My daughter, Bobbi Kristina, has given me *The Greatest Love of All.*

- When I sang *I Will Always Love You* from *The Bodyguard,* it became the longest running number one single of all time!

Who am I?

- I grew up in Yukon, Oklahoma.

- I tried to be a Padre.

- My house has *No Fences.*

- I believe that *We Shall Be Free.*

- My favorite numbers are *Sevens.*

21

Garth Brooks

Who am I?

- I'm a U.S. citizen but couldn't vote for President in my hometown.

- My life became a series of soap operas.

- I made Columbia Records history with one of my songs.

- You may know me from Menudo.

- *Livin' la Vida Loca*

Ricky Martin

22

Who am I?

- I have a British accent.

- I took care of children.

- Children call me Mary.

- Children also call me Maria.

- I love to hear *The Sound of Music*.

23

Julie Andrews

Who am I?

- My characters are well-known on Broadway.

- They prowl around at night.

- People adore my South American lady.

- My phantom haunts the opera house.

- Joseph has a very colorful coat.

Who am I?

- We worked as a team.

- You may like to whistle one of our happy tunes.

- The *King and I* didn't live in the *South Pacific.*

- Although neither of us were from there, we both were fond of *Oklahoma!*

- The *Sound of Music* was music to our ears.

25

Richard Rodgers and Oscar Hammerstein

Who am I?

- At age four, I decided I wanted to sing like Whitney Houston.

- My life has been like a *Cinderella* story.

- I starred in my own television series.

- One thing is for sure, *Never Say Never.*

- *Moesha*

Who am I?

- I often sewed my own costumes.

- I was a role model for many Chicana girls.

- I had seven number one singles on Billboard's Hot Latin Tracks chart.

- Most of my music was in Spanish, but one of my popular English titles was *I Could Fall In Love.*

- Before my untimely death, I was a Tejana superstar living in Corpus Christi, Texas.

27

Selena Quintanilla-Perez

Who am I?

- I grew up in a royal country.

- I am known for my talent at the keyboard.

- I have toured with the Piano Man.

- The *Rocket Man* is my nickname.

- I performed for the *Lion King.*

Elton John

28